FACT CAT

MARY SEACOLE

MARY SEACOLE
NATIONAL PORTRAIT GALLERY
2006

Izzi Howell

WAYLAND
www.waylandbooks.co.uk

FACT CAT

Get your paws on this fantastic new mega-series from Wayland!

Join our Fact Cat on a journey of fun learning about every subject under the sun!

First published in Great Britain in 2016 by Wayland
Copyright © Wayland 2016

ISBN: 978 0 7502 9854 4
Dewey Number: 610.7'3'092-dc23
10 9 8 7 6 5 4 3 2 1

MIX
Paper from responsible sources
FSC® C104740
FSC www.fsc.org

Wayland
An imprint of Hachette Children's Group
Part of Hodder & Stoughton
Carmelite House
50 Victoria Embankment
London EC4Y 0DZ

An Hachette UK Company
www.hachette.co.uk
www.hachettechildrens.co.uk

A catalogue for this title is available from the British Library
Printed and bound in China

Produced for Wayland by
White-Thomson Publishing Ltd
www.wtpub.co.uk

Editor: Izzi Howell
Design: Rocket Design (East Anglia) Ltd
Fact Cat illustrations: Shutterstock/Julien Troneur
Front cover illustration by Wesley Lowe
Consultant: Kate Ruttle

Picture and illustration credits:
Alamy: Niday Picture Library 5, Mary Evans Picture Library 15, FALKENSTEINFOTO 17, Amoret Tanner 19; British Library: BLACKWOOD, Alicia – Lady 14; Getty: Print Collector 4, Jim Dyson 20; iStock: Linda Steward 7, duncan1890 9 and 11, Deborah Maxemow 13b; Shutterstock: catwalker title page and 21, Peteri 6l and 10b, pterwort 6r, Glock 8b, Everett Historical 12, MSPhotographic 13l, LongkauD 13r, sl_photo 18; Stefan Chabluk 10t; Wellcome Library, London 8t, 16.

Every effort has been made to clear copyright. Should there be any inadvertent omission, please apply to the publisher for rectification.

The author, Izzi Howell, is a writer and editor specialising in children's educational publishing.

The consultant, Kate Ruttle, is a literacy expert and SENCO, and teaches in Suffolk.

FACT CAT FACT

There is a question for you to answer on most spreads in this book. You can check your answers on page 24.

CONTENTS

WHO WAS MARY SEACOLE?

Mary Seacole was a nurse and **businesswoman** in the 19th **century**. She lived and worked in many countries around the world, such as Britain, Panama and Jamaica.

In this **modern** painting of Mary Seacole, she is wearing medals from the **Crimean War**.

Mary Seacole helped many soldiers in the Crimean War. She made medicines for them and set up a hotel where they could buy food and **supplies**.

Life was hard for soldiers in the Crimean War. The weather was cold and they lived in uncomfortable, dirty camps.

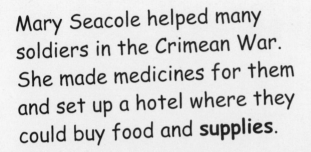

FACT CAT FACT

In the 19th century, some people thought that women shouldn't travel by themselves or have their own businesses, but Mary Seacole disagreed.

CHILDHOOD

Mary Seacole was born in Jamaica in 1805. Her mother was Jamaican and her father was Scottish. Her mother ran a hotel and made **herbal** medicines.

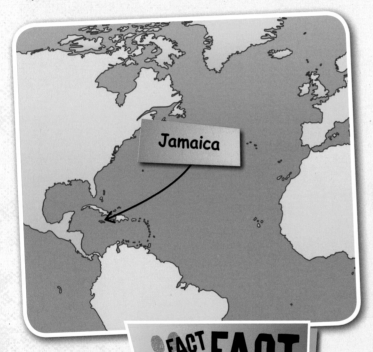

Jamaica

Mary learned about medicine from her mother. She practised nursing her toys and dolls.

FACT CAT FACT

At the time that Mary was born, Jamaica was a part of the British **Empire**. Can you find out the name of another country that was part of the British Empire?

When Mary was 15, she visited Britain. She stayed with her relatives for a year. She made another trip to Britain when she was 18.

Mary Seacole travelled to Britain by ship.

EARLY LIFE

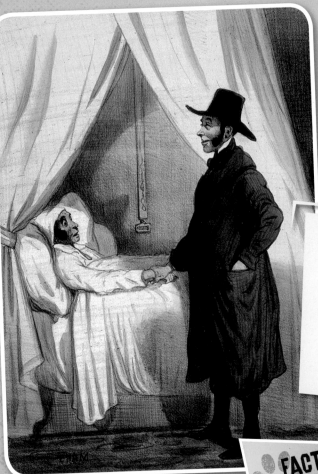

The beginning of Mary Seacole's adult life was hard. Her house in Jamaica burned down. Later, her husband and her mother both died.

In 1850, Mary was in Jamaica when many people became ill with a disease called **cholera**. Do people still get sick from cholera today?

FACT CAT FACT

Mary Seacole watched doctors try to **treat** cholera in different ways. She learned how to treat it with herbal medicines made from mustard and other plants.

In 1851, Mary Seacole moved to **Panama** and started a hotel for gold **miners** who worked in the area. She also prepared food for her guests.

Panama is a **tropical** country in Central America.

THE WAR BEGINS

The Crimean War started in 1853. Britain, France and Turkey fought against Russia. Most of the battles took place in an area called the Crimea.

This modern map shows where the Crimean War took place. Look at the map and name three countries around the Black Sea.

UKRAINE

MOLDOVA

RUSSIA

CRIMEA

ROMANIA

GEORGIA

Black Sea

BULGARIA

Great Britain

TURKEY

Crimea

Some soldiers in the Crimean War were hurt and killed in battle. Others became ill because of diseases and the cold. It was difficult for soldiers to get better in the dirty hospitals.

Soldiers fought with swords and guns in the Crimean War.

FACT CAT FACT

In the Crimean War, more soldiers were killed by illnesses than by fighting. One of the worst diseases was cholera, which soldiers got by drinking dirty water.

GOING TO THE CRIMEA

The British **government** sent nurses to help the soldiers that had been **injured** in the Crimean War. These nurses worked in the British hospitals in Turkey.

FACT CAT FACT

Florence Nightingale was one of the nurses who helped soldiers during the Crimean War. She made sure that the British hospitals were clean and comfortable.

Florence Nightingale was known as the Lady with the Lamp, as she would carry a lamp to check on her **patients** during the night.

Mary Seacole offered to travel to Turkey with Florence Nightingale, but the British government wouldn't let her. She decided to go to the Crimea by herself and set up her own hotel for soldiers.

Seacole brought tins of soup, blankets and saddles to sell to the soldiers. Why did some soldiers need saddles?

THE BRITISH HOTEL

Mary Seacole set up her hotel for British soldiers close to the **battlefields** in the Crimea. She called it the British Hotel.

The British Hotel was a small building made from wood and metal sheets, similar to this drawing. Inside, it was warm and clean.

INTERIOR

FACT CAT FACT

Rats would often eat the food stored at the British Hotel. One rat even tried to eat the finger of a man while he was sleeping!

Soldiers could buy hot meals and supplies at the British Hotel. Seacole also prepared medicines for sick and injured soldiers.

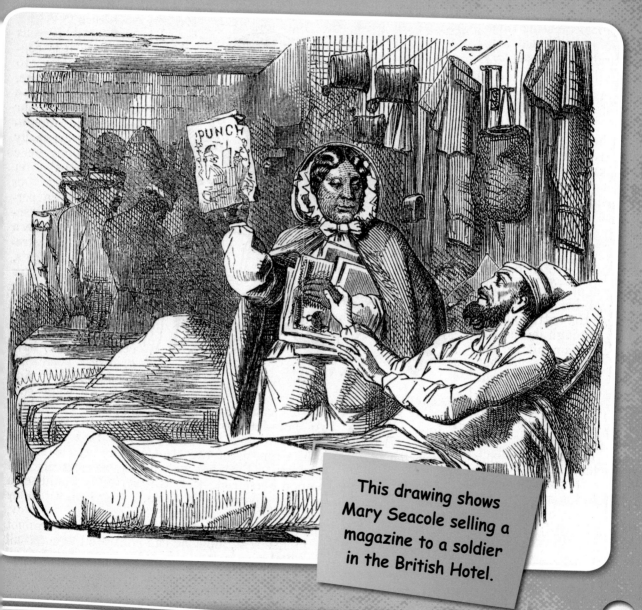

This drawing shows Mary Seacole selling a magazine to a soldier in the British Hotel.

ON THE BATTLEFIELDS

Injured British soldiers had to travel a long way from the battlefields to the hospital. They were taken by boat across the Black Sea from the Crimea to Turkey.

Many injured men died on the journey to hospital. In which Turkish town was the British hospital?

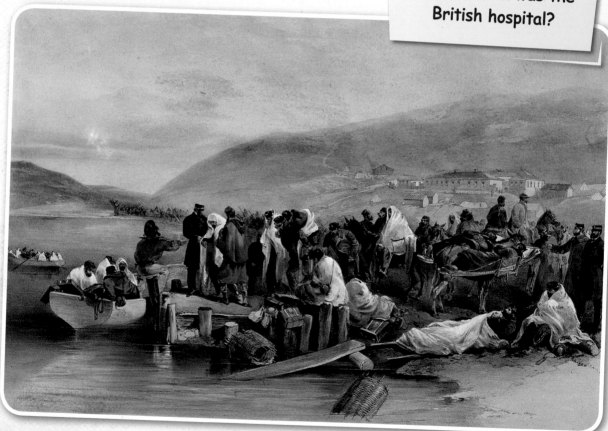

Instead of working in a hospital, Mary Seacole helped soldiers closer to the battlefields. This meant that the soldiers got treatment much faster than those who went to hospital.

The Crimean battlefields were very dangerous. Mary Seacole risked her life to help injured soldiers.

FACT CAT FACT

Mary Seacole treated soldiers kindly. She became known as Mother Seacole.

AFTER THE CRIMEAN WAR

When the Crimean War ended in 1856, Mary Seacole went back to Britain. She didn't have very much money. Soldiers that she had helped in the Crimean War collected money for her.

She gave her aid to all
who prayed,

To hungry, and sick,
and cold:

Open band and heart,
alike ready to part

Kind words, and acts,
and gold.

This is part of a poem about Mary Seacole's work in the Crimean War. What is the name of the poem?

Mary Seacole wanted to share the story of her life with other people. In 1857, she wrote an **autobiography** called 'The Wonderful Adventures of Mrs Seacole in Many Lands'.

This is the only photograph of Mary Seacole. She is preparing herbal medicines in the photo.

LATER YEARS

Mary Seacole didn't travel much after she returned to Britain. She died in 1881 and was buried in London.

Mary Seacole's gravestone is decorated with palm trees as a sign of her Jamaican childhood. How old was she when she died?

HERE LIES
MARY
SEACOLE
1805 ~ 1881

OF KINGSTON, JAMAICA
A NOTABLE NURSE WHO CARED
FOR THE SICK AND WOUNDED IN
THE WEST INDIES, PANAMA
AND ON THE BATTLEFIELDS
OF THE CRIMEA
1854 ~ 1856

Although many people knew about Mary Seacole during her life, she was forgotten for a long time after her death. Today, we remember Mary Seacole for helping many people during the Crimean War.

1st

MARY SEACOLE
NATIONAL PORTRAIT GAL

2006

In 2006, a painting of Mary Seacole was printed on a stamp to celebrate her life.

FACT CAT FACT

Some people think that Mary Seacole was forgotten for many years because of the colour of her skin.

QUIZ

Try to answer the questions below. Look back through the book to help you. Check your answers on page 24.

1 Where was Mary Seacole born?

a) Britain

b) Russia

c) Jamaica

2 Many soldiers in the Crimean War got sick with cholera. True or not true?

a) true

b) not true

3 What did Mary Seacole bring to the Crimea to sell?

a) blankets and saddles

b) gold

c) dolls and toys

4 The British hospital for soldiers was in Russia. True or not true?

a) true

b) not true

5 What kind of book did Mary Seacole write?

a) autobiography

b) cookbook

c) joke book

6 The life of Mary Seacole was forgotten for a long time. True or not true?

a) true

b) not true

GLOSSARY

autobiography a book written by someone about their own life

battlefield a place where a battle is fought

businesswoman a woman who owns a business

century a period of 100 years. The 19th century refers to dates between 1800 and 1899.

cholera a disease that comes from drinking dirty water

Crimean War a war in which Britain, France and Turkey fought against Russia (1853-1856)

empire a group of countries ruled by one leader

Florence Nightingale a British nurse who helped soldiers during the Crimean War

government the group of people that are in charge of a country

herbal made from plants

injured hurt

miner someone who digs rocks and metal out of the ground

modern describes something that is from the present and not from the past

musician someone who plays a musical instrument as their job

Panama a country in Central America

patient someone who is being treated by a doctor or a nurse

supplies food and equipment needed for an activity

treat to care for someone with a disease or an injury

tropical describes a place that has hot, wet weather

INDEX

ANSWERS

Pages 6–20

page 6: Some countries include India, Australia and Canada.

page 8: Yes, people still suffer from cholera in countries that don't have clean water.

page 10: Countries include Romania, Bulgaria, Georgia, Turkey, Ukraine and Russia.

page 13: Because they rode horses in battle.

page 16: Scutari

page 18: A Stir for Seacole

page 20: 75 years old

Quiz answers

1 c - Jamaica

2 true

3 a - blankets and saddles

4 not true – it was in Turkey.

5 a - autobiography

6 true

OTHER TITLES IN THE FACT CAT SERIES...

WAYLAND
www.waylandbooks.co.uk